MASTERING PROMPT ENGINEERING

Enhancing Productivity with GenAI

Kriishna P. Debnath

To my cherished children, Kuldeep and Kamakshi,

Your endless curiosity and unwavering faith have driven my exploration of the vast world of Generative AI. Without you, I wouldn't have been able to discover the endless possibilities that lie within this exciting field. This book is a tribute to your immense impact on my life, and I hope it serves as a constant reminder of my gratitude and affection towards you. Thank you for being my guiding light and pushing me to new heights.

With all my heart,
Krishna P. Debnath.

PREFACE

Generative AI isn't here to replace you; it's your partner in elevation. It's your creative assistant, capable of automating routine tasks, refining your work, and sparking new waves of creativity. By comprehending generative AI, you can harness its potential to amplify your work and productivity.

CONTENTS

INTRODUCTION

During our Thanksgiving dinner last November in 2022, my son, Kuldeep, brought up an interesting topic - ChatGPT. He'd heard about it from his school friends and was excited to share. Naturally curious, I probed him for more details. In simple terms, he explained that ChatGPT was part of something bigger called Generative AI. It had this unique ability to create connections with people.

Intrigued, I dived into the world of ChatGPT in December. I signed up on OpenAI to explore further. Little did I know, this journey would reshape how I think, work and even provide guidance to improve our daily productivity.

While exploring ChatGPT, I discovered a popular concept called "Prompt Engineering." It was a topic of discussion on various platforms such as YouTube, e-learning sites, and podcasts. One day, while in the shower, I began considering how to frame my questions more usefully on ChatGPT. I developed the **PROMPT** framework, which includes the following components: **P**ersona, **R**equest, **O**utput Type, **M**odifier, **P**rovide Example, and **T**one.

◆ ◆ ◆

"Better questions to GenAI yield better responses."

The beauty of GenAI and the PROMPT framework became abundantly clear to me. They were no longer just abstract concepts; they became tools I could use daily. They helped me craft better business cases, user stories, strategic plans, project presentations, and documentation.

Generative AI is a magical technology that allows machines to generate human-like content such as text, images, and music. It's like having a creative assistant at your fingertips, ready to help with any content-generation task. Powered by deep learning models, Generative AI can mimic human creativity and thinking patterns, revolutionizing fields like language translation, creative writing, and problem-solving. Best of all, it's accessible to anyone with the right approach, regardless of technical expertise. This book will explore its immense potential.

The Birth of PROMPT:

As I mentioned, my journey with PROMPT began in a rather unexpected place – the shower. But it wasn't just a random thought; it was the culmination of my curiosity about how to make my interactions with ChatGPT more fruitful.

When I first started using ChatGPT, I often received off-the-mark responses. It wasn't that ChatGPT didn't know its stuff; it was more about how I framed my questions. The realization struck me that the quality of the responses I received depended mainly on th quality of the questions I asked.

So, I began experimenting. I adjusted my queries, refined my wording, and used different styles. And guess what? The responses got better. This experience got me thinking. There must be a structured way to format questions so ChatGPT, or any Generative AI, can provide more valuable information.

And that's when PROMPT came into being. PROMPT is not just an acronym; it's a framework that I developed during one of those shower thoughts. It stands for Persona, Request, Output Type, Modifier, Provide Example, and Tone. These are the key elements that make up a well-structured prompt.

Persona: It's about setting the stage. Who is the AI in this interaction? What's its role or identity? It's like giving AI a character to play in your conversation.

Request: This is the crux of your prompt. What do you want from AI? What's the main point or question you're posing? Being clear and concise here is vital.

Output Type: Specify the format or type of response you're looking for. Is it a detailed explanation, a list, a step-by-step guide, or something else entirely?

Modifier: Context is everything. Adding modifiers helps AI understand the nuances of your request. For example, you might want information about a specific topic within a broader category.

Provide Example: Here's where you show AI what you're expecting. You offer a model response, giving AI a glimpse of the desired outcome. The example of the answer helps AI understand your intent better.

Tone: Set the tone for the conversation. Do you want a formal response, a friendly chat, or something in between? It's about aligning AI's style with your communication goals.

In essence, PROMPT is a recipe for precision. It's a structured way of communicating with Generative AI to get the best possible results.

So, whether you're a student looking to ace your assignments, a professional seeking to streamline your workflow, or simply someone curious about the potential of this technology – this book is for you. It's a practical guide that bridges the gap between GenAI's capabilities and empowering your everyday life.

Are you ready to embark on this journey? Let's dive in and discover the incredible world of GenAI and PROMPT.

CHAPTER 1: UNDERSTANDING GENERATIVE AI

"The true sign of intelligence is not knowledge but imagination." — Albert Einstein

In the age of digital marvels, Generative AI is a wizard, conjuring new content from the boundless depths of data it has imbibed. Imagine it as an artist, inspired by countless masterpieces, creating its unique works of art.

In recent times, generative AI has become a formidable tool, thanks to the advancements in deep learning. This subset of machine learning allows computers to learn from real-world data, making it a more practical and efficient approach than traditional textbook learning methods.

This creative powerhouse of technology extends its influence across a spectrum of domains:

1. Image Generation: Generative AI crafts lifelike images, from photographs that rival reality to artistic paintings that capture the essence of the human spirit. Think about creating virtual worlds, generating marketing materials, or even birthing new forms of visual art.

2. Text Generation: It weaves words together seamlessly, constructing sentences, paragraphs, and entire articles. Imagine the potential for automating tasks such as generating customer support tickets or crafting persuasive marketing copy that resonates with your audience.

3. Music Composition: Generative AI doesn't just play music; it composes it. From catchy melodies to sweeping orchestral masterpieces, it can create entirely new compositions or emulate the style of your favorite artists.

4. Video Production: Filmmakers, Social Media Influencers. Generative AI can produce videos, from short films to animated features. It can create entirely original content or emulate the style of beloved genres.

5. 3D Modeling: Sculptors and designers will delight in their ability to craft intricate 3D models, whether designing products, sculpting lifelike characters, or constructing immersive virtual worlds.

The dynamism of generative AI knows no bounds. It's an ever-evolving field, continually birthing fresh applications. The implications of its power ripple across industries, promising transformative shifts that will redefine how we work, create, and innovate.

Why Generative AI Matters for Modern Professionals

So, why should the modern professional care about generative AI?

1. **Staying Ahead of the Curve:** The landscape of generative AI is ever-changing, with new applications surfacing at a breathtaking pace. To thrive in this dynamic environment, understanding this technology isn't just beneficial; it's

essential. It's the key to keeping you ahead of the curve and prepared for the transformative waves it brings.

2. Enhancing Your Work: Generative AI isn't here to replace you; it's your partner in elevation. It's your creative assistant, capable of automating routine tasks, refining your work, and sparking new waves of creativity. By comprehending generative AI, you can harness its potential to amplify your work and productivity.

3. Problem-Solving: In the face of complex challenges, generative AI can be your ally. Whether generating innovative ideas, crafting intricate product designs, or producing compelling marketing materials, this technology offers solutions to problems that might otherwise appear insurmountable.

Understanding generative AI is paramount for modern professionals aiming to be at the forefront of progress, enriching their work, and unraveling complex conundrums.

Action Items:

1. Begin Your Exploration: Start your journey by delving into the fundamentals of Generative AI. Explore its wide array of applications and understand how it functions. This knowledge will be your compass as you navigate this transformative terrain.

2. Reflect on Your Work: Take a moment to ponder your daily work or ongoing projects. Identify areas where Generative AI could catalyze enhancing your productivity.

Visualize how this technology could streamline your tasks and open new creative avenues.

3. Cultivate Curiosity: Cultivate curiosity as a habit. Generative AI evolves swiftly, with novel applications and breakthroughs emerging regularly. Keep a watchful eye on emerging trends and applications to stay informed and inspired.

4. Record Repetitive Tasks: Here's an additional and equally crucial task: Note down repetitive tasks you regularly encounter. Begin gathering information about these routines, as Generative AI has the potential to become your valuable ally in automating them. Doing so will free up your time for more meaningful and innovative endeavors.

In the upcoming chapters, we will look at Generative AI and its functions, uses, and tips on utilizing it effectively. Get ready to embark on a thrilling adventure of originality, advancement, and change as we uncover the wonders of Generative AI side by side.

CHAPTER 2: THE PROMPT FRAMEWORK

"Clarity of purpose is the driver of every great achievement." - Richard Paul Evans.

The PROMPT Framework: Your Path to Effective Interaction with Generative AI,

As we continue to explore the world of Generative AI, we have been amazed by its incredible creative abilities. To take our exploration to the next level, we can utilize the PROMPT framework, which is a structured approach to crafting communication prompts that are both clear and highly effective when working with generative AI models.

The PROMPT Framework: Demystified

The PROMPT framework comprises six vital components, each serving a unique role:

1. Persona: Imagine setting the stage. Just as in a play, you assign a persona to the AI. This persona defines the AI's role or identity in your interaction. Think of it as giving the AI a character to play in your conversation. For instance, if you seek a creative writing partner, you might endow the AI with a writer's persona. Alternatively, if your aim is research assistance, you might cast the AI as a scientist.

2. Request: The request is the heart of your prompt. It's the pivotal question or point you're asking to the AI. Clarity and conciseness are paramount here. The better you articulate your request, the more effectively the AI understands and responds.

3. Output Type: Specify the format or type of response you desire from the AI. Is it a detailed explanation, a list, a step-by-step guide, or something entirely different? This component helps the AI tailor its response to your expectations.

4. Modifier: Context is everything. Adding modifiers helps the AI grasp the nuances of your request. For example, you might want information on a specific topic within a broader category. Modifiers allow you to fine-tune the AI's understanding to align with your precise intent.

5. Provide an Example: This is where you illuminate the path for the AI. You offer a model response, showing the AI what you're anticipating as a result. This step is constructive if your request is intricate or needs help to articulate it clearly.

6. Tone: The tone sets the mood of the conversation. Do you desire a formal response, a friendly chat, or something in between? This component aligns the AI's style with your communication goals, ensuring a harmonious interaction.

Harnessing the Power of the PROMPT Framework

The PROMPT framework is your gateway to effective communication with generative AI models. By following this structured approach, you can craft prompts that are not only clear and concise but also highly effective. This proficiency enables you to unlock the full potential of generative AI and attain your desired outcomes.

Pro Tips For Crafting Effective Prompts

As you begin your journey with the PROMPT framework, consider these additional tips:

- **Be Specific:** Precision is your ally. The more specific your request, the better the AI can understand and fulfill it.

- **Use Keywords:** When possible, incorporate keywords relevant to your request. The keywords help AI hone its efforts and deliver a more pertinent response.

- **Avoid Jargon:** AI models can find jargon perplexing. Opt for plain language whenever possible to ensure clarity.

- **Exercise Patience:** Finding the perfect prompts may require some experimentation. Don't be discouraged if you don't achieve your desired results immediately.

With practice, you'll become adept at crafting effective prompts that maximize the potential of generative AI.

Unlocking the Power of PROMPT: Real-World

Applications

Here are a few examples of leveraging the PROMPT framework for various use cases:

1. Writing a Resume: You can assign the AI the persona of a hiring manager or recruiter. Your request can be for the AI to create a resume highlighting your skills and experience. Specify the output type as a tailored, detailed resume for a specific job application. Use modifiers to indicate the industry or job type. Provide an example of your preferred resume format, and set a formal tone to maintain professionalism.

2. Job Application Assistance: Empower the AI with the persona of a human assistant. Task it with helping you prepare a job application, such as crafting a cover letter or answering interview questions. Specify the output type, whether it's a written document or an audio recording. Use modifiers to tailor your request to the specific job or interview type. Provide an example of a well-structured cover letter or interview answer, and maintain a formal tone for professionalism.

3. Business Case Development: Assign the AI the persona of a business consultant or analyst. Request assistance with a business case, such as identifying a problem, developing a solution, or evaluating a proposal. Define the output type: a written document or a presentation. Use modifiers to specify the business problem or solution type. Offer an example of a model business case, and maintain a formal tone for professionalism.

These examples showcase the versatility of the PROMPT framework. With a dash of creativity, you can employ this structure for many tasks, making it an invaluable tool for enhancing your interactions with generative AI.

We will look closely at prompt engineering and its various aspects in the upcoming chapters. We'll cover its applications, nuances, and practical strategies for utilizing its maximum potential.

Get ready to become an expert in the PROMPT framework, enabling you to unleash your creativity and innovation while interacting with generative AI.

CHAPTER 3: PERSONA — CRAFTING AI IDENTITIES

"The self is not something one finds; it is something one creates." - Thomas Szasz.

Let's explore the 'Persona' component of the PROMPT framework further, based on what we've learned in the previous chapters. The persona gives the AI a character or identity, setting the tone for interacting with it. Similar to how an actor plays a role in a play, defining the AI's persona helps to shape its responses, establish a solid conversation, and achieve your intended goals.

Why Is Persona Important?

1. Contextual Alignment: By defining a persona, you align the AI's responses to a specific context, ensuring the AI's answers are more relevant and tailored.

2. Predictable Responses: A well-defined persona leads to more consistent and predictable responses from the AI.

3. Enhanced Engagement: Crafting a persona makes interactions with the AI more engaging, allowing users to connect better with the AI and making it feel more personalized and less robotic.

Crafting Personas for Specific Tasks

Creating a persona isn't just about labeling the AI. It's about envisioning how you want the AI to assist you. For different tasks, you'd like the AI to embody other characteristics. Here's how you can craft personas for specific tasks:

- **Understand the Task:** Before creating a persona, clearly understand the task. What do you want the AI to achieve? The nature of the job will heavily influence the persona.

- **Visualize the Ideal Helper:** Think about the characteristics of the ideal assistant for the task. For instance, if you're working on financial analytics, you might visualize a seasoned financial analyst with years of experience.

- **Be Specific:** The more specific you are in defining the persona, the better tailored the AI's responses will be.

Examples of Different Personas for Various Contexts

1. Job Application Assistance

- **Persona:** Career Counselor

- **Characteristics:** Experienced, knowledgeable about industry trends, keenly understands what recruiters look for, and offers constructive feedback.

- **Expected response:** "Here's a way to structure your cover letter to make a strong impression."

2. Writing a Resume

- **Persona:** HR Specialist

- **Characteristics:** Familiar with various job roles, understands critical skills required, and has insight into effective resume structures.

- **Expected response:** "Consider highlighting these specific skills at the top of your resume to catch the recruiter's attention."

3.Business Case Development

- **Persona:** Business Consultant

- **Characteristics:** Analytical, has a strategic mindset, understands market dynamics, and offers actionable insights.

- **Expected response:** "To strengthen your business case, you might want to delve deeper into the market trends over the past five years."

Crafting an appropriate persona for AI isn't just a superficial exercise. It's integral to ensuring that your AI interactions are productive, effective, and enjoyable. It's about molding the AI into your desired assistant, advisor, or partner.

Action Plan

- Reflect on the tasks you commonly perform or need assistance with.

- Consider the ideal persona for each task using the guidelines provided.

- Test your crafted personas in real-world AI interactions, refining them as needed based on the responses you receive.

- Always stay curious, and remember: The more vividly you craft your AI's persona, the richer your interactions will be.

Continue on this journey, and in the next chapter, we'll explore further elements of the PROMPT framework, enhancing our mastery over generative AI interactions.

CHAPTER 4: REQUEST – THE ART OF ASKING

Continuing our journey into mastering Generative AI through the PROMPT framework, we move on to the "Request" component. So far, we've learned about crafting AI personas that set the stage for our interactions. Now, let's explore the critical aspect: making the proper requests.

Why Is A Request Important?

Imagine asking for directions. If you mumble, provide vague landmarks, or leave out crucial details, you're less likely to reach your destination efficiently. Similarly, a poorly articulated request can lead to more precise or irrelevant responses with Generative AI.

The Importance Of Clarity

1. Understanding Intent: An explicit request helps the AI understand your intent accurately. Ambiguity can lead to confusion.

2. Efficiency: Well-structured requests save time. The AI can provide a precise answer instead of seeking clarification.

3. Relevance: A precise request ensures that the AI's Response is directly related to your needs, increasing the significance of the information.

The Art of Crafting Effective Requests

Here's a blueprint for formulating requests that yield precise and valuable responses:

- **Start with a Clear Goal:** Before interacting with AI, have a clear goal. What do you want to achieve? This clarity will guide your request.

- **Be Specific:** Specify the details you need. The more specific your request, the more accurate the AI's response.

- **Use Plain Language:** Avoid technical jargon or overly complex language. Clear and straightforward communication is critical.

- **Consider Context:** Think about the context of your request. What information is necessary for the AI to respond?

- **Ask Open-Ended Questions:** When appropriate, ask open-ended questions to encourage more comprehensive answers.

Examples of Effective Requests

1. Job Application Assistance

- **Poor request:** "Help me with my job application."

- **Effective Request:** Please provide tips for drafting a cover letter for a marketing manager's position.

2. Writing a Resume

- **Poor request**: "How do I write a resume?"

- **Effective Request:** "Can you guide me in highlighting my project management skills on my resume?"

3. Business Case Development

- **Poor request**: "Tell me about business strategy."

- **Effective Request:** "Please provide insights on developing a growth strategy for a tech startup."

Let's look at some real-life scenarios where well-crafted requests led to fruitful AI interactions:

Scenario 1: Job Interview Preparation

- **Poor request:** Provide details to prepare for job interview.

- **Effective request:** "Could you simulate a job interview scenario for a marketing role and provide potential questions and ideal answers?"

Scenario 2: Content Creation

- **Poor request:** Create content for my blog post

- **Effective request:** "Can you generate ideas for a blog post on sustainable gardening practices for beginners?"

Scenario 3: Financial Planning

- **Poor request:** Create a family budget

- **Effective request:** "Please help me create a budgeting plan for my family's annual vacation."

As you embark on your journey with Generative AI, remember that the clarity and precision of your requests play a pivotal role in the quality of the AI's responses. By mastering the art of asking, you unlock the full potential of this powerful tool.

Action Plan

- Practice formulating clear and specific requests for everyday tasks.

- Engage with Generative AI using these well-crafted requests to experience firsthand how it enhances the quality of responses.

- Reflect on your interactions and note any improvements in the relevance and accuracy of AI-generated content.

- Stay curious and refine your request-formulation skills; it's essential to leveraging Generative AI effectively.

Our upcoming chapter will concentrate on the essential element of specifying the "Output Type" and how it influences the reactions generated by Generative AI.

CHAPTER 5: OUTPUT TYPE – TAILORING RESPONSES

As we journey deeper into the world of Generative AI and the PROMPT framework, we arrive at the crucial component of "Output Type." Just like an artist selects the canvas and medium for a masterpiece, specifying the output type shapes the responses we receive from AI.

Why Does Output Type Matter?

Imagine ordering a meal at a restaurant. You don't just ask for "food"; specify if you want a salad, a burger, or a pizza. Similarly, detailing the desired output type is essential when interacting with Generative AI. It ensures that the AI provides the information in a format that best suits your needs.

Significance Of Specifying Response Types

1. **Relevance:** Different tasks require different output types. Specifying the kind ensures that the AI's Response directly applies to your assignment.

2. **Clarity:** It prevents misinterpretation. If you need a visual representation, asking for an image rather than text

eliminates ambiguity.

3. Efficiency: The right output type saves time. If you need data, receiving paragraphs of text could be more efficient.

Exploring Output Formats

Let's take a closer look at various output formats you can specify:

- **Text:** Suitable for written information, explanations, or textual data.

- **Images:** Ideal for visual content, diagrams, charts, or any information that can conveyed visually.

- **Data:** Specifying data output is crucial for numerical or structured information.

- **Audio**: For tasks involving voice assistants or auditory content, audio output type is essential.

How Output Type Influences AI Generated Content

Your choice of output type shapes the AI's Response. Here's how it works:

- **Text Output:** If you specify text output, the AI will provide information in written form. For instance, if you ask for a summary of a news article, you'll receive a written summary.

- **Image Output:** When you request an image output, the AI will generate visual content. If you ask for a chart showcasing sales data, you'll receive an image of the graph.

● **Data Output:** Specifying data output will result in numerical or structured information. For instance, if you need statistical data on market trends, the AI will provide it in a data format.

Examples of Specifying Output Types

1. Job Application Assistance

- Request: "Could you provide a visually appealing template for a cover letter?"

  - Output Type: Image

  - Expected Response: An image of a cover letter template.

2. Writing a Resume

- Request: "Please generate a structured list of my skills and qualifications."

  - Output Type: Data

- Expected Response: A spreadsheet with your skills and qualifications.

3. Business Case Development

- Request: "Could you illustrate the SWOT analysis with a chart?"

  - Output Type: Image

- Expected Response: An image containing the SWOT analysis chart.

Specifying the output type is like customizing your order at a restaurant. It ensures that the AI provides information in the most helpful format. By understanding this aspect of the PROMPT framework, you can further enhance the relevance and effectiveness of AI-generated content.

Action Plan

• Practice specifying output types for different tasks. • Engage with Generative AI using various output type requests to experience how it influences the content you receive.

• Reflect on your interactions and note the impact of choosing different output types on the quality of AI-generated responses.

• Keep experimenting and refining your ability to specify the most appropriate output type for each task.

The next chapter will explore how modifiers can add depth and context to your interactions, making your AI conversations even more effective.

CHAPTER 6: MODIFIER – CONTEXT MATTERS

Welcome to our next chapter on Generative AI and the PROMPT framework. Today, we will discuss using "Modifiers" and how they can help you add more depth and accuracy to your interactions with AI. These modifiers work similarly to adjectives and adverbs, giving your AI persona a more specific tone and personality that can help you achieve your desired goals. Let's dive in and explore how you can use modifiers to enhance your AI interactions.

Continuing The Conversation

In our journey, we've discussed Persona, Request, and Output Type – essential components of the PROMPT framework. Now, it's time to introduce Modifiers. Imagine them as the delicate brushstrokes an artist uses to add depth and detail to their masterpiece.

The Role Of Modifiers

Modifiers play a pivotal role in guiding AI to understand the context and constraints of your request. They are the bridge between what you ask and what you truly intend.

How Modifiers Enhance Responses

1. Contextual Clarity: Modifiers provide context. If you're seeking "climate change" information for a research paper, specifying "current data on climate change" ensures you receive the most relevant information.

2. Precision: They sharpen the focus. For instance, asking for "recent trends in smartphone sales in Asia" instead of just "smartphone sales" narrows the response to precisely what you need.

3. Customization: Modifiers allow you to tailor AI responses to your preferences. Modifiers enable this customization, whether you want a formal tone, a specific style, or a particular depth of analysis.

Strategies For Effective Modifier Usage

- **Be Specific:** The more specific you are in your modifiers, the more accurate the AI's Response will be. If you need information on "digital marketing," consider specifying the time frame, industry, or region to refine your request.

- **Consider Constraints:** Consider any limitations or constraints to your request. For example, if you want marketing strategies for a small budget, specifying this constraint ensures you get relevant suggestions.

- **Style and Tone:** Modifiers can also shape the style and tone of the response. If you're seeking advice for a formal report, modifier like "formal tone" can set the right expectations.

Examples Of Modifiers In Action

1. Job Application Assistance

- **Request:** "Could you formally respond to a job interview question?"

- **Modifier:** Formal Tone

- **Expected Response:** A well-structured, formal response suitable for a job interview.

2. Writing a Resume

- **Request:** "Please generate a creative and engaging summary of my professional experience."

- **Modifier:** Creative Style

- **Expected Response:** A summary that not only lists your experience but does so engagingly and creatively.

Modifiers are the tools that refine your AI interactions, ensuring that you receive responses that align precisely with your needs and preferences. You can take your AI conversations to the next level by effectively mastering the art of using modifiers.

Action Plan

- Practice incorporating modifiers into your AI requests for various tasks.

- Experiment with modifiers like tone, style, depth, and constraints to understand how they impact AI responses.

- Reflect on the quality and relevance of AI-generated

content

when using modifiers compared to requests without them.

- As you continue your journey through this book, keep honing your modifier skills to make your AI interactions more productive and tailored to your goals.

In the upcoming chapter, we'll explore the power of providing examples in your prompts. This skill can significantly enhance the clarity of your communication with AI.

CHAPTER 7: PROVIDE EXAMPLE: SHOWING THE WAY

Welcome back to our journey through Generative AI and the PROMPT framework. This chapter explores the art of "Providing Examples" and how it can be your guiding light in interactions with AI.

Continuing The Conversation:

Our exploration has taken us through Persona, Request, Output Type, Modifier and their vital roles in crafting effective prompts. Now, we reach a crucial juncture – the component known as "Provide Example."

The Value Of Providing Examples

Think of this component as a beacon that illuminates the path for AI. When you provide an example, you offer AI a tangible model of your expectations. It's akin to saying, "Here's what I mean."

How Examples Improve AI Comprehension

1. Clarity: Providing an example eliminates ambiguity. It ensures that AI understands your request accurately. For instance, asking for a "marketing plan" can yield varied results, but specifying "a marketing plan for a new tech product launch" paints a clear picture.

2. Contextualization: Exemplars anchor AI in a specific context. If you want information on "sustainable agriculture," an example like "recent developments in vertical farming techniques" provides the context you desire.

3. Complex Requests: When your request is intricate, providing an example simplifies comprehension. For a difficult task like "writing a technical manual for a software product," sharing a sample section from another manual sets the tone and structure.

Examples of Using Provide Example

1. Job Application Assistance

- **Request:** "Can you help me draft a compelling cover letter?"

- **Provide Example:** Share a well-written cover letter from a previous successful job application.

- **Expected Response:** AI crafts a cover letter in a similar style and tone.

2. Writing a Resume

- Request: "Please create a resume highlighting my project management skills."

- Provide Example: Offer a sample resume section that showcases your project management achievements.

- Expected Response: AI generates a resume emphasizing your project management expertise.

3. Business Case Development

- Request: "I need a persuasive business proposal for a new product launch."

- Provide Example: Share a section of a previous successful product launch proposal.

- Expected Response: AI crafts a persuasive proposal with a similar approach.

Providing examples is a potent tool in your AI communication toolkit. It elevates the clarity of your requests, ensuring that AI comprehends your intent accurately. By mastering the art of offering exemplars, you enhance the quality of AI-generated content.

Action Plan

- Practice incorporating examples into your AI requests for various tasks.

- Experiment with simple and complex examples and observe how they impact AI responses.

- Reflect on the quality and relevance of AI-generated content when using examples compared to requests without them.

As we progress in this book, continue honing your ability to provide clear examples, enhancing the effectiveness of your AI interactions.

In the upcoming chapter, we'll explore the importance of setting the right tone for your AI conversations and how it can significantly influence the quality of AI responses.

CHAPTER 8: TONE: SETTING THE RIGHT MOOD

Welcome to another exciting chapter on the PROMPT framework and Generative AI. This chapter will explore the fascinating concept of "Tone" and its significant influence on AI interactions.

Continuing The Conversation:

Our journey through the PROMPT framework has brought us to the aspect of "Tone." Just like a skilled conductor guides an orchestra, the tone you set in your AI interactions directs the harmony of the conversation.

The Importance of Tone in AI Interactions

Imagine receiving a heartfelt message from a friend and imagining the same news delivered with a formal, robotic tone. The words may be identical, but the emotional impact vastly differs. Tone matters in AI interactions for several reasons:

> **1. Clarity:** The tone you use can clarify your intent. Is it a casual chat or a formal request? Your chosen tone guides AI in understanding the context.

> **2. Engagement:** The right tone can engage your AI

companion more effectively. It sets the mood for a productive and enjoyable conversation.

3. Relevance: It helps AI generate responses that align with your communication goals. For instance, a friendly tone might be suitable for brainstorming ideas, while a formal style suits professional documents.

Aligning Tone with Communication Goals

1. Formal Tone: This is suitable for professional documents, reports, or when seeking concise, factual information. For instance, if you're requesting a market analysis, a formal tone ensures clarity and precision if you're requesting a market analysis.

2. Friendly Tone: A warm tone encourages creativity and engagement in more relaxed conversations or brainstorming ideas. Imagine discussing project ideas with AI as a familiar collaborator.

3. Neutral Tone: Sometimes, a neutral tone is ideal, especially in scenarios requiring balanced, unbiased responses, like research or news summaries.

Case Studies: Tone in Action

1. Job Application Assistance

- **Request:** "Can you help me prepare for a job interview?"

- **Tone:** Friendly and supportive.

- **Result:** AI provides interview tips and conducts mock interviews with a warm, encouraging demeanor.

2. Writing a Resume

- **Request:** "Craft a professional resume for me."

- **Tone:** Formal and precise.

- **Result:** AI generates a resume with a clear, business-like tone, highlighting skills and experiences effectively.

3. Business Case Development

- **Request:** "I need a persuasive business proposal."

- **Tone:** Professional and persuasive.

- **Result:** AI creates a compelling proposal with a tone that resonates with potential investors.

Tone is a powerful tool in your AI interactions. You can enhance clarity, engagement, and relevance by aligning it with your communication goals. Mastering setting the right mood in your conversations ensures more fruitful interactions with AI.

Action Plan:

- Practice adopting different tones in your AI interactions to observe their impact on responses.

- Reflect on how tone influences the quality of AI-generated content and its alignment with your goals.

- Experiment with combining the various PROMPT

components with different tones to create well-rounded, effective prompts.

- As we progress, continue refining your ability to set the right tone for diverse AI interactions, ensuring each conversation achieves its intended purpose.

Our next chapter will explore real-world examples of prompt engineering and its transformative potential across various domains.

CHAPTER 9: PRACTICAL APPLICATIONS

"Knowledge is of no value unless you put it into practice." –
Anton Chekhov.

In the world of Generative AI, understanding is just the first step. The real magic happens when this knowledge is applied practically to solve real-world challenges. This chapter will explore how prompt engineering, specifically the PROMPT framework, offers a transformative approach to various professional scenarios.

Prompt Engineering Across Industries

The evolution of Generative AI, underscored by prompt engineering, has precipitated transformative shifts across diverse industries. By harnessing the power of tailored AI communication, organizations can generate precise, value-driven outputs that enhance efficiency, innovation, and user experience.

1. Healthcare:

- **Crafting Patient Communication:** Personalized patient

interactions are paramount in healthcare. With prompt engineering, healthcare providers can offer individualized advice, reminders, or counseling, ensuring the patient feels acknowledged and understood.

● **Generating Reports:** Patient data and diagnostic results can be overwhelming. Through prompt engineering, AI can distill this vast information into structured, comprehensive reports, aiding in faster diagnosis and treatment.

● **Synthesizing Research Insights:** Medical research is vast and continually evolving. With AI's capacity, new research can be rapidly synthesized, compared, and contrasted, accelerating the pace of medical advancements.

2. Finance:

● **Tailoring Investment Strategies:** Every investor has unique needs and risk appetites. Prompt engineering enables the creation of bespoke investment strategies, optimizing returns while aligning with individual investor profiles.

● **Producing Financial Analyses:** In the dynamic world of finance, timely and accurate analysis is crucial. AI can rapidly parse complex financial data, making comprehensive studies that aid decision-making.

● **Automating Customer Service Inquiries:** With the volume of financial inquiries rising, AI-driven customer service, guided by prompt engineering, ensures that clients receive rapid, accurate, and personalized responses.

3. Education:

• **Curating Lesson Plans:** Every class has its unique rhythm and needs. Prompt engineering allows educators to craft lesson plans tailored to their student's specific requirements and progress, ensuring optimized learning outcomes.

• **Automating Grading:** The grading process can be labor intensive and subjective. AI, structured by prompt engineering, can offer objective, consistent, and swift grading, allowing educators more time to focus on teaching.

• **Providing Tutoring Assistance:** Students often require personalized attention. AI-driven tutors, refined by prompt engineering, can offer students tailored assistance, ensuring their doubts and challenges are addressed.

4. Entertainment:

• **Scripting for Movies:** The world of cinema thrives on novelty. With prompt engineering, AI can craft unique, compelling scripts, offering fresh narratives that captivate audiences.

• **Generating Music:** Music transcends boundaries. AI, guided by precise prompts, can compose resonating melodies catering to diverse genres and moods.

• **Designing Game Levels:** The gaming industry demands constant innovation. Leveraging prompt engineering, AI can create intricate game levels, ensuring engaging and challenging experiences for players.

Prompt engineering, as an integral facet of Generative AI, is not just a technological marvel but a tool reshaping industries, driving efficiency, personalization, and innovation. As we delve deeper into the age of AI, the precise crafting of prompts will play a pivotal role in determining the quality and applicability of AI outputs, making it an indispensable skill for the future.

Success Stories: The PROMPT Framework in Action

- **Navigating Corporate Ladders:** We recently had the pleasure of assisting an executive from a Fortune 500 company with their job application and interview process. Using the PROMPT framework, we created a compelling application and resume that effectively highlighted their credentials, achievements, and personal narrative. The framework allowed us to craft clear, concise, and persuasive prompts that helped the executive articulate their experiences and aspirations in the best possible way. As a result of this process, the executive not only had a polished resume but also walked into their interviews with newfound confidence. We are pleased to report that this approach led to a successful career move that the executive was delighted with.

- **Revolutionizing Work Processes:** Utilizing the PROMPT framework throughout my professional journey, I can attest to its incredible value in streamlining work processes. For example, tasks typically span several months, such as developing business cases or user personas, could be completed in a few days, thanks to the framework's clarity and precision. In one of my projects, we were tasked with drafting a detailed business plan. By leveraging the PROMPT framework, we were able to define our needs meticulously and obtain accurate, comprehensive content from the AI, significantly reducing our project timeline. Overall, the PROMPT framework has revolutionized how I approach work and deliverables, resulting in greater efficiency and quality.

Lessons Learned From Practical Applications

- Iterative Learning: No tool is perfect. The key is iterating and refining. Each interaction with the AI using the PROMPT framework offers insights for subsequent interactions.

- Flexibility is Crucial: While the PROMPT framework provides a structure, it's essential to remain adaptable. Different scenarios may require adjusting the approach slightly to obtain the best results.

- Collaboration Over Solo Efforts: Engaging in prompt engineering as a team or with another individual often yields better results. Multiple perspectives can refine the process and outcome.

The practical implications of the PROMPT framework are vast and varied. Its potential to revolutionize tasks and enhance productivity across industries is immense. However, like any tool, its effectiveness lies in its application.

Ethical Considerations and Potential Risks

While Generative AI and the PROMPT framework offer remarkable opportunities to enhance productivity, it's crucial to recognize that this technology is not without its ethical considerations and potential risks. As you embark on your journey to harness the power of GenAI, it's essential to be mindful of these aspects.

Ethical Considerations:

- **Bias and Fairness:** Generative AI models learn from vast datasets that sometimes contain biases. It's essential to be vigilant and ensure that the prompts and data provided do not perpetuate or amplify these biases. Strive for fairness and inclusivity in your interactions with GenAI.

- **Privacy:** When using GenAI, you may be handling sensitive information. Always be cautious about sharing personal or confidential data, and consider the privacy implications of your prompts and interactions.

- **Transparency:** Some AI models operate as "black boxes," making it challenging to understand their decision-making processes. It's important to seek clarity in AI systems and make informed decisions about the data you provide.

- **Intellectual Property:** If you're using GenAI for content creation or innovation, be aware of intellectual property rights. Ensure that your prompts and interactions comply with copyright and patent laws.

Potential Risks:

• **Misinformation:** GenAI models generate content based on input data. The AI may produce content that perpetuates falsehoods if the input is inaccurate or misleading. Always verify information obtained from AI-generated responses.

• **Overreliance:** While GenAI can be a valuable tool, overreliance on it can lead to reduced critical thinking and creativity. Use GenAI as a complement to your skills, not a replacement for them.

• **Security:** Be mindful of the safety of your prompts and interactions. Unauthorized access to AI-generated content or data breaches can have serious consequences.

• **Quality Control:** AI-generated content may vary in quality. It is essential to review and refine the output to ensure it meets your standards before final use.

As you explore the practical applications of GenAI and the PROMPT framework, remember that responsible and ethical use of this technology is paramount. Stay informed about evolving ethical guidelines and best practices in AI, and always prioritize ethical considerations and risk mitigation in your AI interactions.

By embracing the opportunities and challenges of Generative AI, you can navigate this transformative technology with confidence and integrity, ultimately reaping its many benefits while mitigating potential risks.

Action Plan

● Reflect on your professional and personal tasks. Where can you integrate the PROMPT framework for better efficiency and outcomes?

● Experiment by crafting prompts for diverse scenarios. Note the successes and areas of improvement.

● Engage colleagues or friends in a prompt engineering session. Collaborate, discuss, and refine your approach.

● Stay curious and keep iterating. The landscape of Generative AI is ever-evolving; staying updated and adaptable is critical.

As we move to our subsequent chapters, we'll dive even more deeply, equipping you with advanced strategies and insights for prompt engineering. The adventure continues!

CHAPTER 10: THE FUTURE OF PROMPT ENGINEERING

"The future depends on what you do today." - Mahatma Gandhi.

Welcome to the last chapter of our fantastic journey into the world of Generative AI and prompt engineering. You've made significant progress, and now it's time to look ahead to the exciting future of this ever-evolving field.

Emerging Trends in Generative AI

As we look toward the future of Generative AI and prompt engineering, we must explore some emerging trends shaping this dynamic field. While this book provides a comprehensive foundation, staying up-to-date with these trends will empower you to leverage the full potential of GenAI.

> **1. Enhanced Multimodal Models:** Generative AI models have shown remarkable improvement in managing various forms of data, such as text, images, and audio, concurrently. As a result, this creates more prospects for developing AI-driven applications that are both interactive and captivating in various industries.

> **2. Ethical AI and Fairness:** There's a growing focus

on making AI models fair and ethical. Initiatives to reduce biases and ensure fairness in AI-generated content are gaining momentum as responsible AI development becomes a global priority.

3. Customization and Fine-Tuning: Users are gaining more control over AI models, allowing them to fine-tune models for specific tasks. This trend enables greater personalization and adaptability in GenAI applications.

4. Collaboration and Co-Creation: Collaborative AI models are rising, where humans and AI work together to generate content. This approach fosters creativity and innovation across domains.

5. Natural Language Understanding: Generative AI models are evolving better to understand context, nuances, and user intent, leading to more context-aware and human-like responses.

6. Edge AI: AI models are increasingly being deployed on edge devices like smartphones and IoT devices, enabling real-time AI interactions without heavy reliance on cloud computing.

7. AI-Generated Art and Creativity: AI-generated art, music, and other creative works are gaining popularity, blurring the lines between human and AI creativity.

8. AI in Healthcare: Generative AI plays a significant role in healthcare, from drug discovery to medical image analysis, offering potential disease diagnosis and treatment breakthroughs.

9. AI Assistants and Chatbots: AI-powered virtual assistants and chatbots are becoming integral in various industries, providing personalized customer support, streamlining workflows, and enhancing user experiences.

10. Green AI: With a focus on sustainability, AI researchers are developing energy-efficient AI models and training methods to reduce the environmental footprint of AI technologies.

By watching these emerging trends, you can stay at the forefront of Generative AI and prompt engineering. The future promises exciting developments transforming how we work, communicate, and innovate with AI. As you embark on your GenAI journey, remember that adaptability and a willingness to explore these trends will be valuable assets.

The Evolution of Prompt Engineering

Prompt engineering actively advances within the broader realm of Generative AI. Here are the dynamic shifts we anticipate:

1. Interface Upgrades: Developers will streamline prompt engineering interfaces, creating user-friendly environments. This enhancement will empower even those with minimal technical knowledge to easily craft effective prompts. Imagine a world where professionals can effortlessly instruct AI systems to generate precise responses regardless of their technical expertise. This accessibility will democratize the potential of Generative

AI, making it a valuable tool for various industries and professionals.

2. Refinement of AI Models: As AI models grow more industry-specific, professionals will fine-tune the PROMPT framework and prompt engineering techniques to match. This precision will raise their overall efficacy. Consider a future where AI models are robust and finely tuned to excel in specific domains. For instance, AI will be expertly equipped in healthcare to interpret medical data and assist healthcare providers. In finance, it will specialize in generating precise financial forecasts. This specialization will produce more accurate and reliable AI responses, revolutionizing various sectors' operations.

3. Emphasizing Ethics: Developers will prioritize responsible AI application, ensuring it upholds ethical standards, protects privacy, and minimizes biases. In our pursuit of progress and innovation, we must always keep ethical principles and never compromise them. Developers will put ethical considerations at the forefront of AI development. They will ensure AI respects user privacy, avoids perpetuating biases, and adheres to rigorous ethical standards. This commitment to responsible AI will foster trust and acceptance in society.

4. Championing Continuous Learning: The fast-paced evolution of AI demands unending learning and adaptation. Professionals and AI systems will consistently embrace and adapt to new knowledge, ensuring they remain at the forefront of the domain. In the world of AI, learning never stops. Professionals will continually update their skills to harness the latest advancements. AI systems will continuously learn from user interactions, becoming more proficient with every interaction. This dedication to continuous learning will drive innovation and excellence in prompt engineering.

With the future of prompt engineering intertwined with the broader developments in Generative AI, embracing these proactive changes and committing to ethical and efficient practices will define our journey in this technologically advancing era.

As you conclude this book, I want to leave you with a few parting words:

- **Stay Curious:** The world of Generative AI is an ever-evolving landscape. Keep exploring, stay curious, and embrace the changes it brings.

- **Collaborate:** Engage with others in the field. Share your knowledge, experiences, and challenges. Collaboration accelerates progress.

- **Adapt and Apply:** Prompt engineering is a tool for enhancing productivity. Experiment, adapt, and apply it in your professional and personal life.

Throughout this book, you have embarked on a journey from the fundamentals of Generative AI to becoming a skilled and efficient engineer. You have acquired the skills to shape AI responses, create personas, and utilize the PROMPT framework to achieve outstanding outcomes. Now that you possess this knowledge, you're well-equipped to navigate the thrilling future of AI.

As you close this chapter, remember that the possibilities with prompt engineering are limitless. By using the proper prompts and AI tools, you have the potential to revolutionize your productivity and enhance your quality of life. The future is yours to shape.

Action Plan

- Keep an eye on emerging trends in Generative AI. Stay informed about new developments and applications in the field.

- Continue refining your prompt engineering skills. Practice, experiment, and collaborate with peers.

- Apply what you've learned in this book to your daily work and personal life. Seek opportunities to leverage prompt engineering for enhanced productivity.

- Share your knowledge. Inspire others to explore the world of Generative AI and prompt engineering.

With these steps, you'll be at the forefront of this transformative technology, using prompt engineering to unlock new possibilities and empower your journey toward greater productivity and success.

Thank you for joining me on this enlightening adventure into prompt engineering. Your journey has just begun!

CHAPTER 11: CASE STUDY 1 - JOB APPLICANT

Leveraging The Prompt Framework For Resume Rewriting And Job Applications

The case study explores how Chris Walker, an IT professional with over a decade of experience, leveraged the PROMPT framework to redefine his professional narrative, rewrite his resume, and tailor his job applications amidst a rapidly evolving job market. Recognizing that his old resume lacked the flair and precision needed for the current job market, Chris sought a strategy to stand out.

The PROMPT framework helped Chris in addressing the challenges he faced. He envisioned his resume and job applications as if they were speaking on behalf of a 'Tech Innovator and Leader' persona to highlight his forward-thinking approach, leadership capabilities, and depth in IT. Chris focused on roles within tech firms at the forefront of integrating AI and cloud computing, ensuring his resume and applications resonated with his target employers.

The Prompt Framework To The Rescue:

Having heard about the PROMPT framework, Chris was keen on applying it to his job search journey.

1. Persona: Chris envisioned his resume and job applications as if they were speaking on behalf of a 'Tech Innovator and Leader.' This persona would highlight his forward-thinking approach, leadership capabilities, and depth in IT.

2. Request: Chris sought to communicate his value proposition clearly: "Showcase my expertise and achievements in IT, emphasizing my adaptability and leadership."

3. Output Type: For the resume, Chris needed a chronological format highlighting his career trajectory. For job applications, tailored cover letters emphasizing fit and value for each specific role.

4. Modifier: Chris focused on roles within tech firms at the forefront of integrating AI and cloud computing. This specificity ensured his resume and applications were tailored to resonate with his target employers.

5. Provide Example: Chris studied standout resumes within his industry, deriving a clear sense of what made them compelling.

6. Tone: He maintained a confident, assertive, yet humble tone, avoiding overused jargon and spotlighting tangible achievements and contributions.

Using the framework, Chris rewrote his resume, replacing generic job descriptions with specific accomplishments and quantifying results wherever possible. He also tailored each job application to address the specific needs and challenges of the prospective company. The result was a success rate of securing interviews with four major tech firms, two of which progressed to offer stages, within a month.

As demonstrated by Chris's success, the PROMPT framework can offer a distinct advantage to job seekers. By meticulously addressing each element of PROMPT, job seekers can present themselves in the best light, tailor their applications effectively, and increase their chances of landing their dream job.

Please use these prompts in ChatGPT or any other GenAI to practice the PROMPT Framework.

1. Resume Rewriting:

- Persona: Career Coach

- Request: Revise my resume to highlight my critical skills and achievements.

- Output Type: Provide a well-structured document with clear headings and bullet points.

- Modifier: Focus on tailoring it for a marketing manager position.

- Provide Example: Share a sample resume format for reference.

- Tone: Maintain a professional and persuasive tone.

2. Job Application:

- Persona: HR Specialist

- Request: Assist me in creating a compelling cover letter for a Marketing Manager role.

- Output Type: A well-articulated cover letter that showcases my qualifications and enthusiasm.

- Modifier: Tailor it to match the specific job description and company values.

- Provide Example: Include a model cover letter highlighting key points

- Tone: Maintain a formal and engaging tone.

CHAPTER 12: CASE STUDY 2 - DEVELOPING A BUSINESS CASE

Jane Mitchell, an operations manager at XYZ E-Commerce Inc., a rapidly growing startup specializing in tech gadgets, faced an exciting yet challenging opportunity. The company's board had expressed keen interest in expanding its operations into international markets. Jane, tasked with preparing a comprehensive business case to support this endeavor, recognized that she needed to leverage the power of Generative AI and the PROMPT framework to ensure the success of this ambitious expansion.

Problem Statement: XYZ E-Commerce Inc. is considering expanding its operations into international markets. The management seeks a well-structured business case that assesses the feasibility of this expansion and provides actionable insights to guide decision-making.

Prompt Framework For Business Case Development:

1. Persona: To kickstart the project, Jane created a persona for the AI to emulate. She envisioned an experienced business analyst, someone well-versed in market expansion strategies, capable of conducting in-depth research and crafting data-driven narratives.

2. Request: Jane explicitly requested the AI: "Assist in analyzing the feasibility of expanding our e-commerce operations into international markets and create a comprehensive business case report."

3. Output Type: Jane required a comprehensive business case report to define the output type. This report should include market research, financial projections, and a detailed risk assessment.

3. Modifier: Jane added modifiers to narrow down the focus of the AI's analysis. She specified that the AI should primarily consider the feasibility of expansion into three target regions: Asia, Europe, and South America.

4. Provide Example: Jane offered an example of a well-structured business case outline. This included an executive summary, market analysis, financial forecasts, risk assessment, and an implementation plan. This example was a reference for the AI to understand the structure and content expectations.

5. Tone: Jane set the tone for the business case report as professional and data-driven. She wanted the AI to maintain a corporate style throughout the document, ensuring it aligned with the standards expected by the company's board.

Methodology:

With the PROMPT framework, Jane allowed the AI to initiate the analysis. The AI began by conducting extensive market research on the target regions—Asia, Europe, and South America. It gathered data on market trends, consumer behaviors, competition, and regulatory environments. The AI then used this data to generate comprehensive market analysis sections for each region within the business case report.

Financial projections were the next focus. The AI employed sophisticated financial modeling techniques to forecast revenue, expenses, and profitability under different expansion scenarios. It also factored in potential risks and uncertainties, aligning with the risk assessment modifier.

The AI then structured the report as outlined in the provided example. It crafted an executive summary highlighting key findings and in-depth market analyses for each target region. The financial forecasts were presented, and risk assessments were thorough and data-backed.

Results:

Jane received the AI-generated business case report well within the expected timeframe. The report exceeded expectations in its depth and detail. It provided actionable insights into the feasibility of expanding into the specified regions. The financial projections and risk assessments were particularly valuable for decision-makers.

This case study illustrates how the PROMPT framework, when utilized effectively, can streamline complex tasks such as business case development. By providing clear guidelines to the AI, Jane ensured the production of a comprehensive and data-driven report that was pivotal in the board's decision to expand XYZ ECommerce Inc. into international markets.

Please use this prompts in ChatGPT or any other GenAI to practice the PROMPT Framework.

Persona: Define the AI's persona as a seasoned business analyst with expertise in market expansion strategies. This persona should excel in conducting market research, financial analysis, and crafting data-driven narratives

Request: Clearly express the AI's task: "Assist in assessing the feasibility of expanding our e-commerce operations into international markets and produce a comprehensive business case report."

Output Type: Specify the required output as a detailed business case report. The report should encompass sections on market research, financial projections, and a thorough risk assessment.

Modifier: Add modifiers to specify the scope of the analysis. In this instance, focus on the target regions for expansion: Asia, Europe, and South America. These modifiers provide context for the AI's research efforts.

Provide Example: Present a model business case outline as an example. This outline should encompass sections like an executive summary, market analysis, financial forecasts, risk assessment, and an implementation plan.

Tone: Set the tone for the report as professional and data driven, aligning with the corporate style and the need for a rigorous assessment.

CHAPTER 13: CASE STUDY 3 - LAUNCHING A NEW BUSINESS VENTURE

John Rogers, a driven and innovative entrepreneur, embarked on the exhilarating journey of launching his startup, driven by a groundbreaking product idea. This case study delves into John's entrepreneurial voyage, where he leveraged the power of Generative AI and the PROMPT framework to transform his vision into a thriving business.

Background:

John Rogers, a visionary entrepreneur, was armed with an innovative product idea that had the potential to disrupt an industry. However, he faced the daunting task of transforming this idea into a profitable business venture. John's journey began with a vision but needed a more structured roadmap to navigate the complexities of entrepreneurship.

Challenges:

1. **Concept to Reality:** Converting an abstract product concept into a tangible business proposition requires meticulous planning.

2. Market Dynamics: Identifying the target market, understanding customer needs, and assessing market competition was critical for success.

3. Resource Allocation: Allocating resources efficiently, securing funding, and outlining a clear financial strategy were paramount.

4. Strategic Marketing: Crafting a compelling marketing strategy to penetrate the market effectively posed a significant challenge.

The Prompt Framework For Starting A New Business:

1. Persona: John adopted the AI persona of a seasoned startup mentor with a broad range of experience across various industries. This persona was his guiding light, providing insights, expertise, and invaluable advice.

2. Request: John precisely structured his AI's request: "Guide me through the comprehensive process of launching a new business startup plan. This plan featured: venture. This should encompass market research, business plan creation, and funding strategies."

3. Output Type: The output specified was a detailed, step-by step business startup plan. This plan included comprehensive financial projections, in-depth market analysis, and a strategic marketing blueprint.

4. Modifier: John introduced industry-specific modifiers to tailor the AI's responses to his startup's niche. These modifiers included tech, food, and fashion, providing contextual relevance to his unique business proposition.

5. Provide Example: John leveraged a model businessplan, closely aligned with his industry niche, as a reference point. This Example served as a foundation for crafting his startup plan.

6. Tone: John set the tone for the AI's responses as supportive, informative, and encouraging. This ensured that he received actionable insights, motivation, and confidence in his entrepreneurial journey.

Results:

With the guidance of Generative AI powered by the PROMPT framework, John Rogers meticulously crafted a comprehensive

- Thorough market research that identified target demographics, market trends, and potential competitors.

- A detailed business plan that outlined the company's mission, vision, revenue model, and organizational structure.

- Financial projections, including revenue forecasts, expense management strategies, and funding options.

- A strategic marketing plan encompassing branding, advertising, and customer acquisition strategies.

John's journey from idea to enterprise exemplifies the transformative potential of Generative AI and the PROMPT framework in entrepreneurship. By harnessing the AI's insights, he navigated the complexities of business startups and gained the confidence and knowledge to transform his vision into a successful reality.

Lessons Learned

- The structured PROMPT framework is a powerful tool for entrepreneurs, providing a systematic approach to business planning.

- when channeled effectively through the PROMPT framework, Generative AI can serve as a knowledgeable mentor, offering guidance and expertise.

- Precision and clarity in AI requests result in more valuable and actionable insights.

- Industry-specific modifiers are invaluable for tailoring AI responses to the unique needs of a startup.

Recommendations:

John's entrepreneurial journey serves as an inspiration

for aspiring business owners. Leveraging Generative AI with the PROMPT framework can be a game-changer. Entrepreneurs are encouraged to embrace this technology and embark on their transformative journeys toward business success.

This case study explores how John Rogers utilized Generative AI and the PROMPT framework to launch a successful startup, providing a practical example of how these tools can benefit entrepreneurs in various industries.

CHAPTER 14: CASE STUDY 4 – GENERATING INNOVATIVE PRODUCT IDEAS

A seasoned product manager at a leading consumer goods company, Emma Turner faced the exhilarating challenge of conceptualizing fresh and innovative product ideas for an upcoming product line. This case study delves into Emma's creative journey, harnessing the potential of Generative AI and the PROMPT framework to fuel her product innovation endeavors.

Background:

Emma Turner's role as a product manager demanded continuous innovation and an ability to identify consumer trends that would shape the future of consumer goods. The task was to generate unique and market-relevant product ideas to captivate consumers and set her company apart from competitors.

Challenges:

1. **Market Dynamics:** Understanding dynamic market trends, consumer preferences, and emerging niches requires meticulous analysis.

2. Creativity and Innovation: Fostering a culture of creativity and innovation within the product development team was essential.

3. Competitive Differentiation: Identifying product ideas that would differentiate her company's offerings and resonate with target demographics was challenging.

4. Market Research: Conducting comprehensive market research to validate the viability of innovative product concepts was vital.

The Prompt Framework For Product Idea Generation:

1. Persona: Emma configured the AI's persona as a creative ideator with a rich background in consumer product development. This persona served as her source of inspiration, aiding her in her ideation processes.

2. Request: Emma's AI request was meticulously crafted: "Assist me in generating a range of innovative product ideas for our upcoming product line, taking into account evolving market trends and consumer preferences."

3. Output Type: The output specification was precise—an extensive list of product ideas. Each idea was accompanied by a brief yet insightful description, potential target demographics, and a concise competitive analysis.

4. Modifier: Emma introduced relevant modifiers to spotlight specific market trends. These modifiers directed the AI's focus toward sustainability and digital integration, aligning product ideas with emerging market dynamics.

5. Provide Example: To articulate her expectations vividly, Emma presented a model product idea, complete with a detailed description. This Example served as a reference point, ensuring that the AI comprehended her creative vision.

6. Tone: Emma set the tone for AI responses as creative and forward-thinking. This encouraged the generation of ideas that transcended conventional boundaries and inspired innovative thinking.

Results:

Leveraging the power of Generative AI guided by the PROMPT framework, Emma Turner achieved a breakthrough in product idea generation. The outcomes included:

- A diverse range of innovative product concepts tailored to emerging market trends.

- Detailed descriptions of each idea, offering insights into their potential market appeal.

- Identification of potential target demographics for each product concept.

- Competitive analysis highlighting critical differentiators of each product idea.

Emma's journey from idea inception to innovation exemplifies the transformative potential of Generative AI and the PROMPT framework in product management. By engaging with AI as a creative partner, she identified unique product concepts and instilled a culture of innovation within her team.

Lessons Learned:

- The PROMPT framework and Generative AI catalyze imagination and creativity.

- Clarity in AI requests is paramount to achieving valuable and relevant output.

- Specific market trend modifiers enhance AI responses, aligning ideas with emerging consumer dynamics.

- The creative tone encourages thinking outside the box and fostering innovation.

Recommendations

Emma's experience underscores the value of embracing Generative AI and the PROMPT framework in product innovation. Product managers are encouraged to integrate these tools into their ideation processes, harnessing their potential for disruptive innovation in consumer goods.

This case study illustrates how Emma Turner leveraged Generative AI and the PROMPT framework to revolutionize product idea generation in the consumer goods industry, emphasizing the importance of creativity and forward-thinking in today's competitive market.

CHAPTER 15: CASE STUDY 5 - SUMMARIZING A COMPLEX BOOK REPORT

A diligent high school student, Sarah Anderson found herself amid a challenging assignment: to distill the essence of a multifaceted novel into a coherent, brief book report. Given the novel's intricate plot and deep thematic elements, Sarah sought a structured approach to help her craft a compelling summary without losing the book's nuances.

Background:

Sarah was no stranger to assignments. However, the novel "Eternal Echoes" by L.J. Patterson was unlike any she'd encountered before. A tome blending history, fantasy, and philosophy, it was captivating and complex. Each chapter weaved intricate narratives, and Sarah knew superficial skimming would not capture its depth.

Challenges:

1. **Depth vs. Brevity:** Sarah's primary challenge was to strike the right balance between capturing the novel's depth and keeping the report concise.

2. Thematic Complexities: The novel explored multiple themes, from existential musings to historical intricacies, demanding nuanced interpretation.

3. Character Arcs: The book introduced various characters, each with subplots demanding careful consolidation.

The Prompt Framework For Book Report Summary:

1. Persona: Sarah programmed the AI's persona as "Literary Leo," an expert in literature, particularly familiar with the depths of "Eternal Echoes" by L.J. Patterson.

2. Request: "Literary Leo, assist me in crafting a succinct summary of 'Eternal Echoes,' emphasizing its pivotal plot points, main characters, and overriding themes."

3. **Output Type:** A comprehensive yet concise book report summary suitable for high school presentations.

4. Modifier: Sarah mentioned that her report should encapsulate the essence of the novel's historical elements and philosophical underpinnings.

5. Provide Example: Sarah uploaded a summary of another book she'd written earlier in the year, highlighting her preferred style and depth of analysis.

6. Tone: The summary's tone was set to be educational, analytical, and sufficiently formal to meet the high school assignment's requirements.

Outcome:

With the guidance of "Literary Leo," Sarah crafted a book report that seamlessly blended the novel's intricate plotlines, character arcs, and thematic elements. The summary was concise yet did justice to the book's depth, impressing her teacher and peers

Sarah's journey showcases the PROMPT framework's transformative potential when faced with distilling a complex narrative into a structured summary. By leveraging the capabilities of Generative AI, Sarah achieved academic excellence and deepened her understanding and appreciation of "Eternal Echoes."

Lessons Learned:

- Utilizing the PROMPT framework enables a structured and in depth exploration of literary works.

- Clear and precise requests to the AI ensure alignment with the user's objective.

- Leveraging AI for educational purposes can yield impressive outcomes, enhancing comprehension and analytical skills.

Recommendations:

Students grappling with intricate literary works can significantly benefit from the PROMPT framework. They can transform daunting assignments into insightful academic endeavors by setting clear parameters and harnessing AI's analytical prowess.

This case study sheds light on Sarah Anderson's innovative approach to a high school assignment, demonstrating the efficacy of the PROMPT framework in navigating complex literary analyses.

CHAPTER 16: AUTHOR'S NOTE -THE JOURNEY OF PROMPT ENGINEERING

"Your journey into prompt engineering and Generative AI has just begun, and the possibilities are limitless." – Krishna Debnath.

Let's continue exploring **PROMPT** engineering and Generative AI. We've covered **P**ersona, **R**equests, **O**utput types, **M**odifiers, **B**rovide examples, and Tone.

The book covers persona, requests, output types, modifiers, examples, and tone and how they can enhance productivity in various aspects of your professional life. The practical applications include crafting AI personas for job applications, specifying output types, and setting the right tone. The action plan includes reflecting on how AI can assist you, practicing the PROMPT framework, staying informed, sharing knowledge, and exploring further. The journey never ends, and your productivity is limitless with the proper prompts and AI.

Throughout this book, we've seen how these elements create effective prompts and improve productivity in various aspects of your professional life. Now, it's time to reflect on our journey and the endless opportunities that await.

Thank you for joining me on this expedition into PROMPT engineering and Generative AI. May your AI interactions be ever productive and your curiosity boundless.

Warm regards,

Krishna Debnath.

80

APPENDIX: FURTHERING YOUR JOURNEY WITH GENERATIVE AI

"Learning is a treasure that will follow its owner everywhere." - Chinese Proverb.

Congratulations on reaching the appendices section! As you continue exploring the world of Generative AI and prompt engineering, it's essential to have access to valuable resources to support your ongoing education. This section serves as your toolbox, providing additional reading materials, practice exercises, and helpful vocabulary.

A. Resources for Further Learning and Practice

1. Online Courses

OpenAI Academy: Offers detailed courses on AI concepts and practical applications.

Coursera: Hosts multiple AI and machine learning courses taught by industry leaders.

2. Books

"Artificial Intelligence: A Guide to Intelligent Systems" by Michael Negnevitsky – An excellent foundational text.

"Pattern Recognition and Machine Learning" by Christopher M. Bishop – A deeper dive into AI concepts.

3. Websites/Blogs

Towards Data Science: A Medium publication offering many articles on AI, its use cases, and advancements.

Arxiv.org: A preprint server with cutting-edge research papers on AI.

4. References

Goodfellow, I., Bengio, Y., & Courville, A. (2016). Deep Learning. MIT Press. Russell, S. J., & Norvig, P. (2020).

Artificial Intelligence: A Modern Approach. Malaysia; Pearson Education Limited.

B. Glossary of AI and Prompt Engineering Terms

● Generative AI: Artificial intelligence that can generate new content, such as text, images, or music, based on patterns learned from existing data.

● Deep Learning: A subfield of machine learning that uses neural networks with many layers to learn and make predictions from large datasets.

● Machine Learning: A broader field of AI focused on

creating algorithms and models that enable computers to improve their performance on a task through learning from data.

- Natural Language Processing (NLP): A branch of AI that focuses on the interaction between computers and human language, enabling machines to understand, interpret, and generate human language.

- Persona: In prompt engineering, it refers to defining the role or identity of the AI in an interaction to set the context.

- Request: The core element of a prompt specifies what you want the AI to do or provide.

- Output Type: Determining the format or type of response you expect from the AI, such as text, images, or data.

- Modifier: Additional information added to a prompt to provide context or constraints for the AI's Response.

- Provide Example: Offering a model response or example to guide the AI in understanding your intent.

- Tone: Setting the mood or style of the conversation, whether formal, casual, or friendly.

C. PROMPT Framework Cheatsheet

Persona: It's about setting the stage. Who is the AI in this interaction? What's its role or identity? It's like giving AI a character to play in your conversation.

Request: This is the crux of your prompt. What do you want from AI? What's the main point or question you're posing? Being clear and concise here is vital.

Output Type: Specify the format or type of response you're looking for. Is it a detailed explanation, a list, a step-by-step guide, or something else entirely?

Modifier: Context is everything. Adding modifiers helps AI understand the nuances of your request. For example, you might want information about a specific topic within a broader category.

Provide Example: Here's where you show AI what you're expecting. You offer a model response, giving AI a glimpse of the desired outcome. The example of the answer helps AI understand your intent better.

Tone: Set the tone for the conversation. Do you want a formal response, a friendly chat, or something in between? It's about aligning AI's style with your communication goals.

D. Prompts using the PROMPT framework

1. Resume Rewriting:

- Persona: Career Coach

- Request: Revise my resume to highlight my critical skills and achievements.

- **Output Type:** Provide a well-structured document with clear headings and bullet points.

- **Modifier:** Focus on tailoring it for a marketing manager position.

- **Provide an Example:** Share a sample resume format for reference.

- **Tone:** Maintain a professional and persuasive tone.

2. Job Application:

- **Persona:** HR Specialist

- **Request:** Assist me in creating a compelling cover letter for a Marketing Manager role.

- **Output Type:** A well-articulated cover letter that showcases my qualifications and enthusiasm.

- **Modifier:** Tailor it to match the specific job description and company values.

- **Provide Example:** Include a model cover letter highlighting key points.

- **Tone:** Maintain a formal and engaging tone.

3. Product Idea:

- **Persona:** Product Developer

- **Request:** Generate innovative product ideas for a sustainable travel accessory.

- **Output Type:** Provide a list of creative and eco-friendly product concepts.

- **Modifier:** Ensure ideas align with the travel industry's sustainability trends.

- **Provide Example:** Share an example of a unique travel product concept.

- **Tone:** Encourage a brainstorming and creative tone.

4. Summarize a Document:

- **Persona:** Research Analyst

- **Request:** Summarize a 20-page research report on renewable energy trends.

- **Output Type:** Deliver a concise and informative summary in bullet points.

- **Modifier:** Focus on critical findings, emerging technologies, and market projections.

- **Provide Example:** Share a sample summary of a similar research report.

- **Tone:** Maintain an objective and informative tone.

As you close this book, remember that the journey into AI is continuous and ever-evolving. With the tools and resources at your fingertips, the path ahead is yours to shape. **Happy learning!**

ABOUT THE AUTHOR

Krishna P Debnath

Krishna Debnath is a highly accomplished technology executive hailing from Chicago. With an extensive and diverse background in industries such as Pharmaceutical, Life Science, Automotive, Telecommunication, Retail, Banking, Marketing Technology, and Product Management, he brings a wealth of knowledge and expertise to his work.

In his inaugural book, 'Mastering PROMPT Engineering: Enhancing Productivity with GenAI,' Krishna adeptly unravels the intricacies of Generative AI and prompt engineering, providing readers with invaluable insights to enhance their daily productivity.

He is based in Illinois, where he resides with his loving wife and two wonderful children. Krishna's passion for technology and commitment to sharing knowledge make him an invaluable resource in AI and productivity enhancement.